CUSTOM *Lettering* AND DESIGN SKETCHBOOK